Sailing Away:
A Mother's Final Journey

Walt Kozlowski

Copyright © 2012 Walt Kozlowski

All rights reserved.

ISBN: 0615579043
ISBN-13: 9780615579047

DEDICATION

This book is gratefully dedicated to:
My parents Joe and Mae Kozlowski
for their priceless gifts of love and faith.
My wife Jo Ann for her unconditional love
and unfailing encouragement.
My family for all that they mean to me.

CONTENTS

	Acknowledgments	i
1	Obituary	12
2	Inspiration	14
3	Mother Occupations	15
4	Marriage	18
5	Family Gathering	20
6	Perpetual Prayer	22
7	The Longest Day	23
8	The Last Party	25
9	What's Cookin'	26
10	Whole Faith	28
11	Gift of Faith	30
12	Angelic Gift	31
13	Bedtime 'Bead Time'	32
14	Secret Ingredient	34
15	Friend in Need	35
16	Parental Examples	37
17	They Spell 'Mother'	38
18	Clothed in Love	39
19	True Beauty	40
20	Family Communion	41

21	Caring Caregiver	42
22	Birthday Presence	43
23	Family Comfort	44
24	Calling on God	45
25	Ever Loving	46
26	Different Holidays	47
27	Patience of Job	49
28	Heavenly Food	51
29	Soul Insight	53
30	How's Mae?	54
31	Not-so-secret Ingredient	55
32	Family Resemblance	56
33	Healing Hands	57
34	Godmother	59
35	Love Connection	61
36	Worth by Faith	63
37	Double Dip of Love	64
38	Scarred by Love	65
39	Gift List	66
40	Loud and Dear	68
41	In Their Image	69
42	Wrapped in Prayer	71
43	Skippy	72

44	Joyful Music	74
45	Dance of Love	76
46	Patchwork of Love	78
47	Thinking of Her	80
48	Be It Ever So Humble	82
49	The Kids	83
50	Life's End and Beginning	84
51	One in Love	87
52	Allelujah!	88
	Epilogue	90
	About the Author	91

ACKNOWLEDGMENTS

We are grateful to *The News-Item* of Shamokin, Pa., a Times Shamrock Co., for permission to use the Saturday's Spirit columns as many of the chapters in this book. Special thanks go to Andy Heintzelman, editor, as well as Jake Betz, who approved the creation of the Saturday's Spirit column in 1995.

Our gratitude also goes out to Mother's friends, relatives, JC Penneys colleagues, neighbors, fellow volunteers and all those who took care of her in final illness.

Special thanks are extended to Phyllis Hershey, Mother's cousin who inspired the name for this book, and to Helen Pavis, her best friend.

This book would have not been possible without the cooperation and inspiration of my siblings and their spouses, niece and nephews, as well as the extended Kozlowski-Sadusky families.

Words are inadequate in expressing our appreciation to those whose lives were blessings to Mother – and her family.

INTRODUCTION

My Mother, Mary "Mae" Krouch, was born 2 years after her cousin Phyllis Krouch. As neighbors, Mae and Phyllis were as close as sisters as they grew up. They played together and socialized together. They even walked over two mountains to go swimming at a farmer's public pool and then walked back, making sure to get home before Phyllis' Dad returned from the mines.

Both found jobs with the government; Phyllis after she was graduated from Mount Carmel High School in 1942 and Mae after her 1945 graduation from Mount Carmel Catholic High School. Phyllis met her future husband Harry Hershey and the settled in suburban Harrisburg, while Mae moved back to Mount Carmel and eventually met and married Joseph W. Kozlowski.

The cousins kept in touch with occasional notes, cards and visits throughout their busy years of raising their families. Sadly and eventually, both of their husbands passed away.

Phyllis and Mae exchanged visits. Sometimes, they were purely social as they played innumerable games of two-handed pinochle, and talked and laughed frequently. Other times, Mae would visit to help Phyllis as she recovered from surgery. Phyllis returned the favor.

In 2007, the year my Mother would turn 80, she underwent a double-knee replacement in February, followed by rehabilitation. Her goal was to be ready for a trip of a lifetime – a cruise to Alaska with Phyllis. My Mother had visited 48 states with my Dad and added the 49th, one of the Dakotas, on a bus trip later.

In June 2007, she walked pain-free up the gang plank with Phyllis as the embarked on their trip. It was better than either of them could have imagined, with the company as spectacular as the scenery.

The following April, Mother was diagnosed with a brain tumor during an emergency room visit. Her spirit and spirituality were strong enough to live 18 months more even as her physical health deteriorated drastically and dramatically.

Throughout those many months, Phyllis sent dozens of cards and notes. Most of them recounted old times, told of what was going on in Phyllis' life, mentioned how Phyllis' friends were praying for Mae and stated how sorry Phyllis was about her cousin's plight.

A note written by Phyllis on July 30, 2009, the day after her 84th birthday, expressed surprise that she had lived that long.

It concluded with:

"Take care. I love you. I wish we were on a boat sailing away."

This book is a collection of memories of Mae Kozlowski's final journey, and a bit of where and how she traveled through the first 80 years of her life.

FOREWORD

This book is told from my prospective, but any member of my immediate family could have written one. My wife Jo Ann and I were fortunate to live next door to my Mother for 14 years and we were only 2 miles away when we moved into our new home.

We were blessed by having daily contact with my Mother. We were also the only local family members during Mother's illness.

However, my brother Phil, his wife Helen and son Greg; my brother Dave, his wife Holly and their children Christian and Claire; and my sister Mary Jo and her husband Holden all made different and important contributions to Mother's well-being.

Each of them provided Mother with something she needed – a visit, a smile, a prayer.

We were all united as a result of our love for Mother.

1 OBITUARY

No matter how lengthy and comprehensive an obituary is, it provides only the most basic of portraits of a person's life. Mother's obituary was no exception. She was a person who enjoyed family and friends, loved to laugh and make others laugh, and to help others. Her obituary is nothing more than a few brushstrokes of the painting that was her life.

Mary P. "Mae" Kozlowski

MOUNT CARMEL – The poet Bessie Anderson Stanley wrote that a person "who has lived well, laughed often, and loved much" is a success. By those measures, Mrs. Mary P. "Mae" Kozlowski was an unqualified success.

Mrs. Kozlowski, 82, formerly of 234 W. Second St., Mount Carmel, died Sunday, Nov. 15, 2009, at 9:45 p.m. in St. Catherine's Medical Center, Fountain Springs, where she had been a patient since Jan. 18. She had been in ill health for a year and a half. Even while she was ill, she still retained her ever-present smile and her ready laugh.

Born in Mount Carmel, on Sept. 4, 1927, Mrs. Kozlowski was the daughter of the late Stephen and Mary (Graham) Krouch. She was a 1945 graduate of Mount Carmel Catholic High School. She worked part-time as a clerk at JCPenneys in Mount Carmel until it was closed in 1991.

She was married June 9, 1948, in Church of Our Lady Rectory, to Joseph W. Kozlowski, who preceded her in death Sept. 29, 1996. A loving wife and Mother, she was a great cook and a skilled seamstress. Her home was continuously filled with the sound of her lovely soprano voice singing old standards as she carried out a myriad of tasks. One of those songs, "The Song Is Ended but the Melody Lingers On" is particularly appropriate in describing her passing.

Mrs. Kozlowski was active in the Democratic Party, serving one term as Mount Carmel Democratic Party chairperson and many years as a committeewoman. She was elected to four four-year terms as Mount Carmel Borough assessor. She also served as a member of Northumberland County Housing Authority. She was a familiar to voters in Mount Carmel 1-1, first as a committeewoman and later as assistant constable.

Mrs. Kozlowski was one of the original members of PEPPI exercise group at Family Home Medical, Mount Carmel, and an active participant for 11 years. She was a longtime volunteer deliverer of Meals on Wheels in Mount Carmel, and "pierogie pincher" at SS Peter and Paul Ukrainian Catholic Church, Mount Carmel. She was involved in the crafts group at Mount Carmel Area Senior Citizens Center. She also belonged to the Ladies Auxiliary of the Fourth Degree of the Knights of Columbus.

A deeply religious woman, she was a member of Divine Redeemer Church, Mount Carmel, where she served for more than 10 years as a special minister of the Holy Eucharist. She traveled extensively with her husband and on numerous charter tours. A cruise to Alaska with her cousin Phyllis Hershey in 2007 enabled her to have visited every one of the 50 states.

Survivors include four children and their spouses, Walter J. Kozlowski and his wife Jo Ann, Den-Mar Gardens, Philip S. Kozlowski and his wife Helen, Yorktown Heights, N.Y., David R. Kozlowski and his wife Holly, West Chester, Ohio, and Mary Jo Kozlowski and her husband Holden Butt, Sonestown, and three grandchildren, Christian, Claire and Gregory Kozlowski. In addition to her husband and parents, she was preceded in death by a sister, Marcia A. Krouch, in 2006.

Stanley concluded her poem by noting a success is someone "whose life was an inspiration; whose memory a benediction." Mae Kozlowski was such a success.

2 INSPIRATION

When it came time to write the obituary for Mother, it was difficult to do justice to 82 full years in a matter of a few paragraphs.

I think God was responsible for the inspiration to use the poet Bessie Anderson Stanley's sentiment that someone "who has lived well, laughed often, and loved much" is a success. They perfectly suited the successful life of Mae Kozlowski

Six months later, my wife Jo Ann, her Mother and I were eating a Mother's Day meal at a local restaurant. There were plenty of empty tables and booths, but Jo Ann steered us to a table for four near the rear.

The empty seat at our table was a silent yet potent reminder that it would be our first Mother's Day without my Mother.

A moment or two later, I looked up at the decoration behind the empty chair. It was a plaque, bordered by grapes and it contained the following words, "Live well. Love much. Laugh often."

The words were in slightly different form, yet God was responsible for the inspiration. It reaffirmed the faith that those we have loved and lost will be found with God by us some day.

+++
God inspires us in countless ways.

3 MOTHERLY OCCUPATIONS

Even faced with torture, some people would be more likely to reveal state secrets than to tell their true age. Mother, Mary "Mae" Kozlowski, had no such qualms.

Sometime didn't believe her when she told them that her odometer had moved past 70, 75 and then 80 years. She had the energy and appearance of someone 20 years younger.

I was not around for her first 27 years and the first couple years after my birth are kind of hazy, but I can provide commentary after my 6th or 7th birthday. Even so, it is still difficult to categorize my Mother or what she did.

Cook is the first term that comes to mind. This was back when coffee was instant but everything else wasn't. You also have to keep in mind she was trying to feed me, my two brothers and sister. Trying to keep four kids fed is equivalent of trying to fill in the Grand Canyon a tablespoon of dirt at a time.

My Mother cooked for quality as well as quantity. Just thinking about the meals she whipped up has my mouth watering to the extent that I am in danger of electrocuting myself by drooling on my computer, so I'll move on.

Cooking and cleaning up the aftermath of meals were enough to keep three hard-working non-Moms busy 12 hours a day. My Mother not only did that; she also found time to sing as she worked

Her lovely soprano voice could be heard coming from the kitchen at any hour of the day. A good voice proved to be only partially inheritable. My brothers and sister all have pleasant voices, but when I sing I sound like a 12-year-old garbage disposal choking on a chicken bone.

The profession of town crier is supposed to have gone out of existence a couple of centuries ago, but my Mother was living proof that it was still alive. At least a dozen or two times a day, she would go out on the front or back porch to call which one of us was AWOL.

You were pretty much expected to ignore the first two or three calls, but when the volume of her voice doubled and she started calling out our first, middle and last name, we knew she meant business.

I don't know what would have happened if she had to call again, but I know I didn't want to find out.

That brings me to another one of her roles – disciplinarian. My Dad was often away at summer school, so my Mother was left as the only person standing between us and a small-scale riot. At times, she must have felt like someone armed with a licorice whip and water pistol being sent into a cage full of lions.

If one of the little lions, however, went too far the lion had a good chance of being sent to his room without his supper or – in extreme cases – getting to eat his supper but having to eat standing up.

My Mother was often called to play the role of nurse. This generally meant applying a small dab of mercurochrome and large dabs of tender loving care. But we kids didn't have it easy. If she was out grocery shopping, sometimes we would have to wait a half hour or more before she got home and we could start crying.

Seamstress was another one of her jobs. My Mother's sewing talent guaranteed my sister was often sporting a new dress. Since I rarely wore dresses (I preferred pants suits), I didn't usually benefit much from this talent.

However, it paid off during my hippie ears when she ended up sewing patches on top of patches on my jeans. When I walked down the street, I looked as though I was wearing a bell-bottom quilt.

As we got older, our Mother got even more titles. Our mom – like most moms – was always a worrier, but she moved up to a new level of worrying in our teen years.

When we were little, she used to wake up early because she was worried because we wouldn't get to school on time and she wanted to make sure we were out of bed. Years later, she wouldn't go to sleep until the last one of us was home and safely in bed.

And as we grew older, our Mother was able to go back to a paying job so she became known was of the friendly clerks at Penney's. Even after the store had been closed for a decade or more, she perplexed people who could not quite place where they met her. All it took was for her to say the magic word "Penney's" and the look of confusion was replaced by a smile of recognition.

She added politician to her portfolio when she became a Democratic committeewoman and eventually town chairman. She also served four terms as town assessor. Like her singing, though, her electability was not inherited. I could run unopposed and still come in third.

The same could be said for her fondness of travel. My Mother always had one suitcase packed in case a trip came up. She was on so many bus trips, AAA called her when they wanted to know how to get someplace.

So there you have it. My Mother has been a cook, singer, town crier, disciplinarian, nurse, seamstress, worrier, store clerk, politician and traveler, as well as a couple dozen other things.

Put them all together and they spell "Mother."

In contrast, I am only one thing. Grateful.

+++

**God's love is shown
in what we do for other.**

4 MARRIAGE

Usually, there is a space of a few hours between wedding and reception to permit the taking of pictures of the wedding party. In the case of my parents Joe and Mae Kozlowski, the gap was more like 40 years.

After they got married 60 years ago, on the morning of June 9, 1948, they got in a car and drove nearly 1,000 miles to Alabama for another wedding. My Dad was best man for his best friend from Seabee days during World War II, Russell "Abe" Lincoln.

My folks' wedding reception was a 40th anniversary party staged by my two brothers and their wives, my sister and me. My wife, my sister's husband and my parents' three grandchildren were all in the future, but I like to think they were there in spirit.

The climax of the all-day and late-night gathering of family and friends came that evening when my parents finally performed the wedding reception ritual of cutting the special cake and feeding a bite to each other.

The warmth of that gathering remains among special memories, flickering like the candles that illuminated the tables in the backyard where celebrants socialized.

As with the other events of this life, those sweet memories were followed by bitter ones. It was the last family gathering for Dad's only brother Al, who succumbed to cancer later that year.

Dad was in the early stages of Alzheimer's disease, which eventually claimed his life 2 years before he and Mother would have celebrated their 50th anniversary.

Who knows how our Dad, then 27, and my Mother, then 20, envisioned their future together on their wedding day 6 decades ago.

There were the routine yet special moments; the countless times we gathered around the kitchen table for some of Mother's delicious cooking, or the numberless times we were tucked in and wished, "Pleasant dreams."

There were the joyful memories of the births of their children and grandchildren, the weddings of their children and various graduation ceremonies. Of course, there were the sad ones of the deaths of loved ones and serious illnesses.

All of these were tempered my parents sincere faith in God; reflected in their devotion in church and evident in their actions out of church.

The anniversary party that celebrated the numberless blessings that God had given the family since in the 40 years of marriage was a sublimely sweet occasion.

Who can imagine how sweet the reception will be when the family is together again with God forever?

+++

A marriage with God is cause for celebration.

5 FAMILY GATHERING

Crudely cut-out and colored-in art projects. Perfumed-scented fancy handkerchiefs. Boxes of candy. Greeting cards ranging from Hallmark to marked down.

These were some of the items which my two brothers, sister and I gave to our Mother on Mother's Day when we were kids, and she accepted for what they were – gifts of love.

We've improved in our gift giving in recent decades. This progress is due to the facts that we all have bigger allowances now and we get excellent suggestions from our spouses.

However, when our Mother turned 80 September 2007 and we celebrated at a family luncheon, the best gifts were neither gift wrapped nor gift cards. The old African story of the journey being part of the gift was illustrated there.

My sister Mary Jo and her husband Holden had a 2-hour drive to the restaurant. My brother Phil, his wife Helen and their son Greg made a 9-hour round trip for the 2-hour party. In addition to having several of my mom's cousins as surprise guests, my brother Dave was a long-distance surprise as he flew in from Cincinnati that morning and back that afternoon to represent his wife Holly and their children Christian and Claire, who could not attend.

As I drove home with my wife Jo Ann and my Mother, my pride in my family was surpassed only by the gratitude for my family. We all rejoiced in being a chance in celebrating the life of our Mother – and Father – whose love of us and love of God are the foundation of our lives.

In the spring of 2008, fewer than 7 months after the birthday party, we were jolted by the news that our Mother, who has the energy and enthusiasm of someone 20 years younger, had a serious health problem.

The tense, subdued atmosphere in the surgery waiting room in the hospital bore little resemblance to the festive gathering in the restaurant a few short months before. The one common factor was that Phil had driven in from New York, Dave had flown in from Cincinnati and Mary Jo and her husband Holden had also come there for what turned out to be a 15-hour vigil.

Phil remarked that night that our late Dad would have been proud of the support our family had shown for our Mother. That is no doubt true, but not quite complete.

Our presence during this trying time is similar to the simple Mother's Day gifts of our childhood. Nothing we could do or nothing we could give would be enough to repay the woman who gave us life, made countless sacrifices to make this life better, and showed us through word and example that God's love gives us faith in the present and hope in the future.

+++

**A Mother's love comes
closest to God's love.**

6 PERPETUAL PRAYER

Mother, my brother Phil and I drove the roadway leading the perpetual adoration chapel at SS Cyril and Methodius.

We were all slightly in a daze as we had just come from meeting with the surgeon who would do a biopsy of our Mother's brain the next week to see what type of tumor was there. We were among the many who have made the Danville chapel a stop en route to or from nearby Geisinger Medical Center.

We were not alone. There was an elderly man, who was rapt in prayer when we came in and when we ended our visit.

I didn't ask the man what his story was, but I imagined that he was there – alone with God – because his wife was either in the hospital or had been beyond what the hospital could do.

The latter turned out to be the case for my Mother. The biopsy revealed a tumor that 25 sessions of radiation or several months of chemotherapy could not help.

The best we can do is what the old man did – keeping on praying even if God does not answer our prayers they way that we would like.

+++

It is vital to talk to God;
it is even more vital to listen

7 THE LONGEST DAY

When Mother woke up the morning of Tuesday, April 1, 2008, the day started as it usually did. Once downstairs, she would eat a bowl of oatmeal, drink a cup or two of coffee, say her morning prayers and read the newspaper.

However, this particular morning was far from normal. Slightly slurred speech prompted her to call her doctor's office and she was advised to next call for an ambulance to take her to a hospital.

She left a message for me on my phone at school, so I arrived at the emergency room less than an hour after she got there. The results of an MRI arrived an hour or two later – she had a brain tumor.

Mother's preadmission appointment was for April 4, 2007, and her brain biopsy was moved up from April 23 to Wednesday, April 9. This was a spiritual coincidence since was a novena of prayers from the diagnosis to the biopsy surgery.

She was her usual stoic self in the days leading up to the biopsy surgery, yet there were two matters that preyed upon her mind.

A little more than 2 years before, her younger sister Marcia had died after surgery for lung cancer in the same medical center. Aunt Marcia's heart failed just as the surgeon was telling my Mother and her cousin Ellen how well the surgery had gone.

Then there was a very unsettling coincidence about the surgery. It was 60 years to the day when her Mother Mary died in her late 40s of a cerebral hemorrhage.

Mother and her four children, Phil, Dave, Mary Jo and me, waited in a tense quiet once we arrived at the medical center ahead of her 6:30 a.m. reporting time. It was a while before she was finally called back for pre-op preparations.

When we saw Mother in the pre-op area, her unemotional resolve dissolved in tears. Although she did not question why this was happening to her, she could not help but think about what might happen during the biopsy surgery or what the brain tissue sample would reveal.

We received a pager from an employee at the surgery desk and went upstairs for breakfast, thinking that the biopsy would soon be over. We were still thinking that afternoon when we grabbed a bite for lunch and late that afternoon when we ate something else.

For one reason or another, her biopsy kept getting pushed back further and further on the surgery schedule. It wasn't until early that evening that we got word that the biopsy had been taken and Mother was in post-op.

I was the only one allowed to go to see her in the recovery section. A swath of her always stylish gray hair at the left front of her scalp had been shaved and it bore a bandage. Far more disturbing was the sight of Mother crying.

I will never know whether the tears were ones of relief of having survived the surgery or of fear of what lay in store for her.

All of us were able to be reunited in the dimness of the MRI waiting room at night, and when we briefly visited Mother when she was finally ensconced in her room about 15 hours after she arrived for the surgery.

Despite all that she went through in the next 19 months, I cannot recall another time that she cried.

This was a testimony to Mother's courage, which was result of her love of God and her faith in His will.

+++

**Tears fall to God
as prayers rise to Him.**

8 THE LAST PARTY

We didn't know it then, but the bridal shower proved to be the last official family function that my Mother attended.

The party was held about 6 weeks after she had been diagnosed and after the first week's worth of a series of 30 radiation treatments.

Despite her medical problem, Mother was determined to attend the bridal shower being held for Jennifer, the woman who was marrying Peter, son of her niece and nephew Barbara and Bobby.

Coincidentally, the party took place just a few days after Mother and my sister Mary Jo picked up a wig courtesy of the American Cancer Society and chosen with the help of a very compassionate hair stylist.

A 2-inch wide swath of her hair was cut off for a biopsy done a month before, and it never grew back.

It was the first and only time she would wear the wig, but we didn't know that any more than we recognized this would be final family fete.

When we got home after the 2 1/2-hour roundtrip, Mother was tired but very satisfied. She had had a good time at the shower and enjoyed spending time with family at Bobby and Barb's house before and after the party.

Mother was supposed to attend the wedding in a few months, but she did not make it. She suffered a setback that hospitalized her for a few days and sent her to a nursing home for rehab for 6 weeks.

In the course of 60 years as a Kozlowski, she had attended countless family gatherings. The last one enabled her to enjoy the company and savor the love of at least some members of that family.

+++

Family is second only to God.

9 WHAT'S COOKIN'?

I felt a pang of disappointment when I tried to access my old messages on the phone in the school library where I work. The one that I wanted most was gone. It was Mother telling me not to worry, but she was being taken by ambulance to a hospital emergency room so they could determine what was causing her slurred speech.

We found out that afternoon that a brain tumor and not a stroke was to blame. It seemed important that I preserve that message. I don't know how I would have copied it, but the point became moot because the message was gone.

It wasn't until much later that I realized that the truly memorable phone message Mother was the one she greeted me with nearly every time I called.

"What's cookin'?"

Actually, the phrase conveyed two meanings. The first was an example of her "go-with-the-flow" philosophy she needed when it came to family. Sometimes, I was calling to tell ask her if she would be able to postpone a half hour or so the delicious Sunday dinner she was preparing for us.

When my siblings, their spouses and families would visit, she was fond of using the acronym snafu – situation normal, all fouled up. She handled changes in arrivals and departures with a calm acceptance of the inevitable.

"What's cookin'?" also conveyed her willingness to try new experiences. She was up for a variety of activities. Sometimes, it was to help out as she did with Meals on Wheels and as a "pierogie pincher" for a church (not her own).

Mother had a zest for living that found her getting on buses for various theater productions and sightseeing tours. She also boarded jets to see the sights from Hawaii to Ireland and a cruise ship to take in the beauty of Alaska.

Her deep faith was at the core of this way of looking at and living life. She was grateful to God for the pleasures in her life – whether late-arriving offspring or pleasure trips with friends. It also helped her accept without question her final illness.

In her case, "What's cookin?" was more a matter of "Who's cookin'?" with God being the master chef of the life that she never tired of tasting.

+++

**It's amazing what we
can cook up with God.**

10 WHOLE FAITH

Thirty times Mother made the 38-mile roundtrip from her home to the medical center to receive radiation treatments for her brain tumor. Those came after her initial visit when she was fitted for a mask that she wore during the treatment.

The treatments began in mid-May and were done Monday through Friday, with my Mother getting weekends and Memorial Day off.

Although she was 80 years old, she had possessed the health and vigor of a woman 20 years younger – at least until her world was rocked with the diagnosis of a brain tumor. She tapped into that physical and inner strength when she began her radiation treatments six weeks later.

For the first week or so, she was able to walk from the car to the hospital entrance and then 100 feet to the elevator that took her to the basement where she had another 100 feet or so to go to the radiation oncology department.

However, it did not take long for these arduous treatments to begin to take their toll. By the second week, she needed to use a walker to navigate from the car to the treatment and back to the car.

Within a few days, we had to use a hospital wheelchair to get her back and forth.

As her strength declined, she accepted the progression from walking to using a walker and, finally, to being a wheelchair without comment, much less complaint. She realized what was happening to her was God's will and she accepted whatever help she needed as the treatments progressed.

There was one ritual that did not change in the course of those 30 treatments. We had obtained a temporary "handicapped" placard to hang from the car's rear-view mirror. This permitted us to park close to the hospital entrance, so Mother's trip would be as short as possible.

Once we got in her back in the car after each treatment, the first action she would take would be to reach up and take down that "handicapped" sign.

The tumor and its treatments may have forced her to surrender part of her independence to accept help in getting around.

However, her faith in God was not handicapped by her medical condition.

+++

**God carries us when
we can no longer walk.**

11 GIFT OF FAITH

Praying with a rosary was just as much a part of my Mother's life as eating and sleeping. She had a variety of rosaries, ranging from the worn set of beads once used by her Mother to a beautiful green rosary she purchased on a once-in-lifetime trip to her Mother's ancestral home in Ireland.

The rosaries of this story were the last she acquired. Not long after my Mother was diagnosed with a brain tumor, she had my sister Mary Jo order a rosary from Mother Angelica's EWTN in Alabama. She was very pleased with the beaded prayer aid.

Less than a month later, my Mother had my sister order another rosary from EWTN. However, this rosary was not for her even though she was undergoing a round of chemotherapy and a month's worth of radiation treatments.

The second rosary was for my Mother's friend Verna, who was scheduled to undergo surgery for another form of cancer. My Mother anxiously awaited the mail, hoping to be able to give the rosary to her friend before her life-and-death procedure. She was very happy to get the rosary to her friend before Verna left for the operation.

The rosary gift did not help either woman physically. My Mother died 1 ½ years later. Her friend did not live that long.

However, the spiritual example my Mother left is still alive. If a woman facing her own death can be that concerned about the problems of a friend, what excuse do I have for not expressing my love for God and others in the same way?

+++

**Helping others is
a powerful prayer.**

12 ANGELIC GIFT

We are often called on to buy tickets for various drawings featuring everything from tacky and fabulous prizes or varying amounts of money. We generally consider the purchase a donation to the worthy cause of the organization selling the chances.

There is no telling how many "donations" my Mother made over the decades, but to her pleasant shock she actually won a prize some years ago. The Christmas-themed drawing featured as its top prize a delicate angel with fiber-optic-colored gossamer wings amid a field of poinsettias and holly accented in gold.

It would have looked great in her living room. At least it would have if my Mother had kept the angelic prize. She had put my name and my wife Jo Ann's name on the ticket, so she took great pleasure in making us a gift of the Christmas decoration.

Since then, it has been displayed in a prime location atop the armoire for the television. It complements the gold ornaments and red poinsettias with which Jo Ann beautifully decorates our Christmas tree.

Whenever we gently lift the seraphic scene from its plastic cocoon so we can place it in its holiday setting, we are always struck by the beauty of the angel.

Only it wasn't the angel and the countless gifts that my Mother had given us. It was the love light of the Mother whom God gave my family out of His love.

+++

God gives His Love to us for us to share.

13 BEDTIME 'BEAD TIME'

Except for the month and a half in 2008 when Mother was hospitalized or undergoing rehabilitation in nursing homes, she was able to spend the months after her brain biopsy, radiation treatments and chemotherapy in her own home.

Admittedly, life was vastly different for the 80-year-old woman who had been fiercely self-sufficient. She loved being with her family and friends, but she had also willing been willing and able to live independently.

She thought nothing of driving 3½ hours by herself to visit my brother Phil, his wife Helen and their son Gregory in New York. Likewise, she would drive to Harrisburg Airport to fly out to Cincinnati to visit my brother Dave, his wife Holly and their children Christian and Claire.

Cancer changed her home life dramatically. Once the radiation and chemotherapy treatments started, she needed more and more help in getting through the day. Aides and nurses from Family Home Health Medical proved lived up to their motto of becoming family as they helped her with her meals, medicines and other parts of her daily routine.

Dave, Phil and my sister Mary Jo and her husband Holden were able to help out when they visited.
Jo Ann and I did what we what we could, with Jo Ann preparing many meals that could be heated for Mother. They were but a

small repayment of the many delicious meals Mother had cooked for us over the years.

Mother's bedtime routine did not vary. We would help her into her hospital bed in the living room, and make sure she was covered and that her emergency call button was handy.

The final act was to give her a rosary, which she went to sleep holding.

Mother had quite a few rosaries, including an emerald green one she bought on her trip to Ireland and a crystal one that was once her Mother's and was well-worn from use.

However, the rosary she would take to hospital bed with her was a cheap plastic one.

It proved to be the most precious of all rosaries at that time. Its plastic beads were made dear by the strong faith in God that remained undimmed in a woman facing the end of her mortal life.

+++

**We hold most dear
what brings us closer to God.**

14 SECRET INGREDIENT

My wife Jo Ann and I were helping my Mother bake cookies for what turned out to be Mother's. This means that my mom is supervising, my wife is doing the baking, and I am washing the dishes and trying to stay out of the way.

As I wash the Mirro® cookie sheets that have survived over 45 years of hard use with only a minimum of wear, I think about the thousands upon thousands of toll house, oatmeal raisin and other cookies that have been baked on those aluminum sheets.

Year after year, my Mother has filled several large containers with dozens upon dozens of baked goods. There are enough cookies for unlimited snacking for family and friends, and large bags of takeout tasties for departing guests.

Even with my wife doing most of the work and me helping with the unskilled tasks of preparing, baking and cleaning up, it was a time-consuming process.

How did Mother manage to bake all those cookies the years when my two brothers and I were in our perpetual-motion years? What about those years when she not had to supervise the guys but also look after our younger sister?

After all we kids had left home, the job did not get any easier. For quite a few years, she had to bake while having always to keep an eye on my Dad his Alzheimer's disease took an ever-increasing toll on his body.

As a widow, she continued to crank out the cookies a batch or two at a time despite knees that made each step a painful one. Last year, she got two new knees and turned 80 yet still baked more cookies than ever.

I still don't know how she was able to do all that baking, but I do know why. She did it out of love for us.

We will always have many unanswered questions about Jesus being born to follow His Father's will until it led to the sacrifice of the cross.

But we do know why. He did it out of love for us.

+++
God's love makes life sweeter.

15 FRIEND IN NEED

Before Charlie Brown found his perfectly imperfect Christmas tree and the Grinch had seen the error of his ways, there was Amahl. I don't know what kind of ratings "Amahl and the Night Visitors" got in the 1950s and 1960s, but Gian Carlo Menotti's short opera was a seasonal must-see for my Dad.

It was as much a part of our Christmas as the 6 a.m. sprint down the stairs as my two brothers, sister and I raced to see what Santa had left under the tree. Sometime during the afternoon, Dad would tune into the story of a Mother and her son with a handicapped leg who got around with the aid of a crude crutch.

Their lives changed the day they met the Three Kings, or Magi, who were following the great star on their way to present gifts of gold, frankincense and myrrh to the Christ child. The poor Mother and son had nothing to give Jesus until the boy offered his crutch. Immediately, his leg was cured and the story ended with Amahl and the Magi leaving for Bethlehem to see the Word made flesh.

Last year, decades after Amahl had faded into night, the story on Christmas afternoon involved my Mother, who had been reduced to using a wheelchair to get around as a result of the effects of a brain tumor.

When my wife and I arrived for what was to be my Mother's last Christmas, we discovered she had company, her best friend Helen Pavis. Helen was leaving to spend a week with her daughter, but she had her other daughter bring her to visit mom.

In other words, Helen gave up part of Christmas with her family to spend with Mother.

The tumor had made speaking very difficult for my Mother, so the two friends spent a few hours in the quiet company of each other. They did not have to talk much. Friends can communicate what they are feeling without words.

Unlike Amahl, there was no Christmas miracle for my Mother. She could not walk unaided.

Yet, Amahl in fiction and Helen and my Mother in real life realized that the gold and precious materials are not the greatest gifts we can give. Love is.

Love was the gift that Jesus gave us when He was born in human form 2,000 years ago. God's love for us is the true meaning of His first Christmas.

God's love was the true meaning of the last Christmas for Mother when Helen gave up time with her family to spend it with her friend.

+++

**<center>The more we give our love,
the more we have of it.</center>**

16 PARENTAL EXAMPLES

In a world where some stores start playing Christmas songs in the summer swelter, it is increasing difficult to remember that Christmas is a holy day as well as a holiday.

It's easy to get caught up in the commercialism where the gift is more important than the giving, and the giver's love for the recipient is determined by how much he or she spends on that person. There are some, though, who try to make sure the true importance of the day is remembered.

When I was a kid, the parents of some of classmates had the custom of baking a birthday cake for Jesus on the commemoration of the Savior's birth. For some families, the tradition was to wait until Christmas Eve to have the youngest child place the Baby Jesus in the manger in the family's nativity tableau.

Our Mother concentrated her baking efforts on cookies, and my parents' concern about the nativity set was to see that my brothers and I did not recruit the shepherds and wise men statues to serve as reinforcements for our Union and Confederate toy soldiers.

While assisting Santa, our parents still managed to keep God in focus. Despite staying up late to make sure our presents were in neat stacks under the tree, they also accomplished the near-impossible feat of separating us from our new toys, getting us dressed in "church clothes" and accompanying us to Mass.

But our parents were not flowery church-goers; those who attend church when Easter lilies are on the altar and when the poinsettias of Christmas are in bloom. They attended church every Sunday and made sure we kids did too.

There are also daily examples of their devotion to God: grace said at meals, well-used prayer books and cards, well-worn rosaries, and my Dad's long-standing habit of attending Mass every day.

By their examples and actions, our parents taught us that Jesus is not only "the reason for the season." He and His love are the reason for every season and for eternity.

+++

God is always present as our greatest present.

17 THEY SPELL 'MOTHER'

One of the first words my siblings and I probably uttered was "Mama." However, I can only remember us calling her "Mother."

We were in the minority among our friends who usually referred to their female parent as "Mommy" and then as "Mom." There was even one neighbor who scandalized us by calling her parents by their first names. (My brothers, sister and I did not refer to any adult without out prefacing his or her name with a "Mr.", "Mrs." or "Miss.")

I don't know the reason for my Mother's preference for that for that endearing title, but I know while she may have been Grandma Mae to her grandchildren she is still "Mother" to us.

Over the years, the term had come to embody and sum up all the qualities she possessed and all that she had done for us. Unselfish, funny, conscientious, hard working, giving, forgiving, caring, compassionate, helpful, devoted, devout, loyal, spiritual, practical and a thesaurus-full of adjectives could be applied.

In the end, though, "Mother" for our family and "Mom" for other families could be summarized in one word – love.

Likewise, it would impossible to describe God with a million adjectives, but the Father can be summarized as limitless love without end.

+++

A Mother's love comes closest to God's love

18 CLOTHED IN LOVE

Sifting through envelopes of old family photos, I came across one of my sister Mary Jo as a young girl and my Mother. Each was clad in an identical dress made by my talented sewing Mom.

Mother made dozens of articles of clothing for my sister – not to mention her dolls – over the years. She also displayed her virtuosity and all-around talent at the sewing machine by turning out a Revolutionary War costume for my 6'5" brother and a leisure suit I requested as one of the worst ideas I've had in a lifetime of bad fashion choices.

Back in the days when Memorial Day was always on May 30 even when the holiday did not fall on a Monday, Mother used her sewing skills to make identical brown-print shirts for my two brothers, my Dad and me.

We looked like a Boy Scout troop with a strange fashion sense as we followed tradition and walked a mile or so to the cemeteries to visit the graves of relatives on that long-ago Memorial Day.

Those matching shirts were relegated to rags decades ago, but my siblings and I still wear another outfit sewn for us by our Mother – and Dad – those many years ago.

They clothed us with the love of God that is the primary garment in an ensemble that also includes faith and hope.

Such an outfit was in style then, is now and will be forever.

+++

We are always well-dressed

when we are clothed in love.

19 TRUE BEAUTY

If there is such a thing as a punctuality gene, I surely did not inherit it from Mother. I habitually arrive at events and appointments right on time or wrong on time – late. By contrast, my Mother is always ready to go wherever she wants to go well before time.

She was definitely not like the stereotypical women you see on TV or read about in books; women who are never ready on time. When she and my Dad were going out for a rare evening of socializing, he didn't have to pace up and down like the Fathers on sitcoms. She was ready to go.

A big factor in this is that my Mother has never worn makeup. (At least she didn't in the nearly 55 years that I had known her.) No mascara, no eye liner, no powder, no blush, no lipstick. She just dabs on a couple drops of Jean Naté™ After Bath Splash and she was good to go.

She really did not need a satchel full of cosmetics. When she was feted at a party in honor of her 80th birthday, she looked at least 15 or 20 years younger than what her birth certificate stated. She just had a charismatic glow about her.

If that was true for her face, it was true for her faith. There is nothing ornate or overdone. The rosary, book of prayers and good works were as much a part of her daily life as church attendance was part of every week.

At the center of her life was a love for God and her family and friends.

You don't get much simpler than that – or any more beautiful.

+++

God's love illuminates us from within.

20 FAMILY COMMUNION

The envelope usually arrived in the third week of the month. It contained a schedule for members of our church who assisted at Masses as extraordinary ministers of Holy Communion.

On two, sometimes three, of the Saturday assignments would be found the names of three Kozlowskis, my Mother, my wife and I.

We served as a team for over 10 years, but I never gave it much thought until Mother became ill and could no longer serve. For a year and a half of Mother's illness, my wife and I served with a variety of other special ministers.

We then took the host, which our faith believes is the body of Christ, to my Mother wherever she was, convalescing at home, being rehabilitated at a nursing home, being treated at a hospital and, finally, being cared for in a long-term unit.

After the Saturday evening Mass, we would wait for our pastor to go to the tabernacle to a host to place it in a pyx, a small brass container. He would give us a blessing that we would carry to Mother when Jo Ann and I gave her the host.

It was a special privilege to be able to bring Communion to Mother when she could no longer attend the church that was so important to her spiritual life.

Giving the gift of life to the woman who gave you the gift of life is a soul-stirring blessing.

During the decade or so in which I served with my wife and Mother, I never stopped to think how blessed I was to be able to serve God along with the two women whom I love the most. I do realize that now.

I also realize that in this life or the next, we are never far from those we truly love when we serve as messengers of God's love.

+++

When we serve others, we serve God.

21 CARING CAREGIVER

There were many kind and compassionate people who passed through Mother's life in the 18 months from when her brain tumor was first diagnosed until her death.

One of the most memorable is a physician's assistant named Jessica R. Annis. Mother only met her a half dozen or so times when she visited the hematology oncology department at the clinic while she was receiving chemotherapy after 30 radiation treatments.

In her job, Annis must have seen dozens of cancer patients in the course of a week. I am sure she treated them same as treated Mother – special.

In an age, when people are often rushed in and out of medical appointments, the young physician's assistant was never in a hurry when she came into the examination room for Mother's appointment.

She arrived with a friendly smile and continued with encouraging words. Her concern was evident. Her friendliness and caring attitude were memorable, but her actions late one afternoon were even more so.

Mother had the last appointment that afternoon, so the waiting room was virtually deserted when we were called back to the exam room. It didn't take long for Annis to become concerned about something in Mother's condition.

The PA immediately set up an MRI to confirm or allay her fears. Not only did she make arrangements for setting up in the radiology department downstairs, she accompanied us down for the test and then waited until the results became available.

Fortunately for Mother, Annis' fear proved unfounded and we were able to exit through the empty waiting room.

Even more fortunately for Mother, she had been blessed to have found a care giver like Annis who truly cared about the care she gave.

+++

Compassion for others blesses the bestower.

22 BIRTHDAY PRESENCE

When I was a kid, my approaching birthday brought one thought to mind. Presents! I have since gained a different perspective and it is only fitting that was due to the person who was with me on my original birthday –my Mother.

My brothers, sister and her husband, my wife and I gathered in our Mother's hospital room in early September 2009 to mark her 82nd birthday. As a result of her inoperable brain tumor, it was an occasion that appeared doubtful, at best, when we marked her 81st natal day.

Her very presence was a great gift in itself. Despite the toll the disease has taken on this once-perpetual-motion lady, she still recognized us and enjoyed our company. She still enjoyed eating; particularly ice cream. She was grateful to the aides, nurses and doctor who helped her. She took pleasure in the visits of friends and relatives. She could still find reasons to laugh.

Of course, those were merely the latest in a countless series of blessings that began with the gift of life. She and our Dad gave us our faith in God more by their actions than by their words.

We also received from our parents a sense of humor, respect for ourselves and others, and the belief that money is not the most important priority in life. (It's not even in the top 5.)

As we celebrated our Mother's life of giving, we thanked God for the incomparable birthday gift of our Mother, as well as her gifts of a love of life and a life of love.

+++

God's birthday gift to us is His love.

23 FAMILY COMFORT

Each family operates on the same kind of generational cycle. Elders eventually depart for eternal life while members of the newest generation are born into this life.

Sometimes and sadly, though, this pattern is broken. Such was the case for my cousins' son who had fought a long and valiant battle against brain cancer. He had just turned 40 when he could fight no more.

Since the funeral was to be on a Saturday morning in northern Virginia, my siblings and I made plans to attend. My sister and her husband drove a few hundred miles to attend the viewing Friday evening, and each of my brothers flew in from Cincinnati and New York, respectively, the day of the funeral.

I had a 3 ½-hour ride and one passenger – my Mother. Although it involved a 7-hour roundtrip to get back in time for a late afternoon service at our church, my Mother, a year or so shy of 80, never considered the option of not attending.

When we got to the church, we discovered that she was the only family member of her generation in attendance. In general, she went out of a sense of duty and a feeling of familial love. However, there was one special and specific moment which more than justified her long trip.

This occurred not during the service but at the luncheon that followed. My cousin, the father of the young cancer victim, spotted her and embraced her, his Aunt Mae. She didn't say much; she just hugged him.

As a member of the oldest generation, she was there to provide comfort to her nephew.

We can all take comfort in the knowledge that when our time on earth runs out, we have the opportunity to be joyfully reunited with our loved ones in God's family.

+++

God's love comforts us in sorrow.

24 CALLING ON GOD

339-2074. That's not three three nine-two zero seven four. It's three three nine-two Oh seven four.

As long as I can remember, those were the digits I had to remember if someone asked me what the phone number was at my family's home. My brothers, sister, parents and I must have given out that number thousands of times in a half century or so.

When we ordered takeout, met new friends, registered in doctor's offices and did countless other activities, that was the number we had given.

Then, a few weeks ago, 339-2074 went back on the market. We were closing up the home so we no longer needed the number. We had to inform friends and relatives – not to mention creditors – that the old number was no longer ours. They would have to reach us at other home phone numbers or, more likely, at cell phone numbers.

Inevitably, though, we will miss notifying some people. When they call the familiar 339-2074 they will either be informed by electronic voice that the number is no longer in service or find themselves talking to the new owners of the number, people who never heard of my family and wouldn't know where we were even if they had heard of us.

Some of our friends may never find out the new number to call. It's troubling to realize that. It is somewhat bittersweet that three three nine-two Oh seven four no longer belongs to our family.

It is comforting to know, though, that God will always have our number. He only requires us to pick up the phone of prayer to talk with and listen to Him.

+++

We are all called by God.

25 EVER LOVING

When our family home was sold, my brothers, sister and I found ourselves sifting through over 60 years of memories that began with the marriage of our parents Joseph W. and Mary P. "Mae" Kozlowski.

While our Dad was well-known as the a great acquirer of objects of all shapes and sizes, it turned out that out Mother was a keeper of papers, bank statements and greeting cards of a variety of types.

The cards that each sent other for birthdays, wedding anniversaries and Valentine's Days were of a wide assortment and range, but there was a consistency in the way they signed the cards that spanned the decades.

Dad would invariably sign his cards to Mother as "Your ever-loving husband." Mother's signature was inevitably, "As ever, Mae."

His cards stopped as Alzheimer's disease ate away at his once-brilliant mind. Hers ceased after his death in 1996. Now that Mother has peacefully passed into the afterlife, one thought comes to mind.

Joe and Mae are together again, ever-loving as ever in the presence of God for ever.

+++

**Death is the door by which
we enter God's house.**

26 DIFFERENT HOLIDAYS

Although we share with others holidays and special occasions throughout the year, these observations and celebrations remain uniquely personal.

The most dramatic illustration of the way we personalize these special days in the wake of the death of someone we love without limit. This is most evident in the year the follows the death.

Mother died in November, so my family and I experienced almost immediately what a void her departure would leave in special days. Thanksgiving, the day on which Mother's cooking talents were on grand display, came while we were still numb from her death.

Surprisingly, Christmas was not as bittersweet as expected. When my siblings and I were young, she and our Dad made sure that we remembered Christ is the reason for the celebration and we were beneficiaries of the non-spiritual gifts of the season.

After our immediate family spread out of over three states, our Mother "made the holiday" as schedules were synchronized for all-too-brief get-togethers.

By contrast, March 17, St. Patrick's Day, was more poignant by her absence than the bigger holidays. Her Mother was 100-percent Irish, so our Mother imbued the holiday with ethnic energy.

April 1 was not a time for thoughts of practical jokes. It was on April 1 2007, when she found out in a hospital emergency room that she had a brain tumor, one that eventually claimed her life.

Appropriately, the next day was Good Friday, a spiritually sad day in the best of years. Thankfully, that will be followed by the joy and promise of Easter.

We knew that Mother's Day, her and our Dad's wedding anniversary, and her birthday would lie ahead to test our faith, call for hope and evoke our love.

It helped to keep in mind that we would not have the glory of resurrection on Easter if there had not been the crucifixion on Good Friday.

If her death had ended the love she gave us and the love we had for her, we would have no reason to celebrate, but it did not.

We hold on to the Easter promise that we may reunite with our Mother, Dad and others we hold dear, and we may share an eternity of love with each other and – most importantly – with God.

+++

Each day can
and should be a holy day

27 PATIENCE OF JOB

The Old Testament figure of Job has been the standard of patient acceptance of God's will for many centuries. He loses his vast herds and flocks of animals, he faces the death of his children and he endures the physical pain of his ailments.

Mother was not a Biblical scholar, so the only time she referred to Job was to use to the cliché to show that someone needed the patience of Job to cope with a particular trial.

Her brain tumor affected her speech, with her talking being similar to someone who has undergone a major stroke. In fact, her fateful trip to the emergency room was based on the premise that she had suffered a stroke. That theory was discounted hours later when an MRI showed that there was a brain tumor that proved inoperable.

As the disease progressed, her left side became progressively weaker, necessitating the use of a cane, then walker and finally a wheelchair.

The only time she even mentioned her medical problems was when I was taking her to a nursing home from a hospital where she had been taken when the home health aide could not get her to get up from her chair.

"It all happened so fast," was Mother's sole comment on her medical fate. There was no, "Why?"

As if the tumor were not enough to cope with, she had a brief bout with the painful viral infection known as shingles. On Dec. 31, 2008, we got a call around noon that she had fallen at home.

She began her last new year as a hospital patient recovering from a hip replacement.

That summer, a hospital aide was making Mother's bed and Mother fell to the floor. Hard. The initial diagnosis was that she had broken her neck. Thankfully, her neck was not broken. She still wound up with two black eyes and a cervical collar.

And, her age and condition left her with one more woe – skin tears. Her skin was so delicate that no matter how gently the nurses and aides moved her, she developed bruises and often skin tears.

Despite all the problems, she did not complain and still laughed frequently.

Job eventually passed his test after being admonished and advised by God. He lived to see his wealth restored and to be blessed by more daughters and sons.

Mother's release from her earthly ailments came only with her death. However, she did leave behind for her family and friends a beautiful example of the grace of a soul who has yielded fully to God's will.

+++

**We can bear all
if we yield to God's will.**

28 HEAVENLY FOOD

As a result of her love for family, my Mother could have qualified for any number of jobs – chauffeur, referee, judge and jury, seamstress, counselor and so on. However, she would be best qualified for the position of cook.

She qualified for that by both the quality and quantity of food she prepared for my two brothers, sister, Dad and me over many years. When my brothers and I were in our perpetual eating years, she must have felt like a fireman on a train heaving shovel after shovel full of coal into ever-hungry steam engine.

Cooking for what must have seemed like a regiment or two of hungry paratroopers would have been reason enough to be grateful to her. That gratitude would be multiplied by the fact that she was an excellent cook, with such specialties as Swiss steak, beef stew, macaroni salad and snap-a-doodle coffee cake.

Unfortunately for her, my siblings' and my efforts to make a token repayment did not turn out as well. Every Mother's Day, we would provide her with breakfast in bed featuring food that only a Mother could love.

As adults, we could only make token repayments for all of her gastronomical generosity by treating our Mother to occasional home-cooked or restaurant meals.

It wasn't until her final illness that we had the opportunity to bring to her the perfect food – a host that we believe is the Body of Christ. After Mass every Saturday evening, our pastor would give my wife and me a pyx, a metal container the size of a pocket watch in which we carried the Holy Eucharist.

We would take it to Mother's home, nursing home or hospital and give it to her. At first, I placed it in her hand and she would reverently place the host into her mouth. As she grew weaker, I placed it on her tongue.

The host or Holy Eucharist is also called what Jesus called Himself: "I am the bread of life; he who comes to Me will not hunger, and he who believes in Me will never thirst."

What a tremendous grace, blessing and consolation it was to me to have given "the bread of life" to the woman who gave me life itself. On each Mother's Day, I am reminded that she will never again be in pain or want for anything as she lives forever in the Light of God.

+++

**God provides us
with what we truly need.**

29 SOUL INSIGHT

Mother could have been accurately described as a "shady person," though not in the title's usual definition. Her skin could be termed as the "Whiter Shade of Pale" that the old group Procol Harum used to sing about. As a result, if she ventured outdoors on sunny days she would try to find a seat in the shade.

As her illness progressed, she was outdoors less and less. When she was receiving care at home, virtually the only time she got outdoors was to go to a hospital appointment. Occasionally, one of her children on a visit to her in a nursing home or hospital would take her for some fresh air.

In her final months, her skin became paler and thinner; as fragile as a delicate flower just past its prime.
No matter how careful her care-givers were, they could not avoid giving Mother skin tears. Such spots would bruise and sometimes even lacerate the skin so bandaging would be required.

You could always notice the blue-appearing veins in her hands and wrists, but as the months progressed her lower arms seemed to be semi-transparent as more and more veins became visible.

She reminded you of the transparent body models that are used to show children how blood is the life flow of humans.

The way Mother patiently bore the various pains and inconveniences of her illness demonstrated much more than the core of her physical being.

The faith and patience with which accepted her medical problems displayed the love of God that was at the core of her spiritual being.

+++

Faith is transparent.

30 HOW'S MAE?

One of our last visits with Aunt Jane was also one of the most memorable.

Although she had sailed past her 90th birthday a little more than a half year before, Aunt Jane was coping with a variety of medical problems. My wife Jo Ann and I did not know what to expect when we entered her room.

A week before, Aunt Jane had slept through our visit. Briefly holding Jo Ann's hand was the only recognition she showed.

This time was much different. Aunt Jane was wide awake and greeted each of us with a kiss as we'll bent over her bed.

"Where's Mae?" was the first thing she said. Mae was my Mother. Although she had died well over a year before, she was the first person Aunt Jane always asked about. My aunt's short-term memory was gone, so my Mother still lived on for her.

This time, Aunt Jane said something she had never done before. "Mae. Where are you?" she called out.

Resting on her chest was a stuffed tiger, a gift from one of her grandchildren. After a while, she put the tiger on the right side of the bed and began to try to grab and lift the edge of the bed spread with her right hand.

It took a moment for the purpose of this maneuver to become clear. Aunt Jane took the edge of the blanket to cover the stuffed tiger so it "wouldn't get cold."

After we had kissed her good-bye, Aunt Jane thanked us for coming to see her.

The brief visit epitomized the life Aunt Jane had lived for over 90 years. She loved being with family. She was concerned about others – even asking first about my deceased Mother. She was kind to animals – even stuffed ones. And, she was grateful.

Now, she is reunited with my Uncle Al, her parents and others who have gone on before her. She will even be able to ask Mae in person how she is doing.

+++
God comes first; others come next.

31 NOT-SO-SECRET INGREDIENT

Most good cooks have dishes for which they are noted. My Mother was certainly in that category with her talent at making such specialties snap-a-doodle coffee cake, beef stew, and baked, breaded chicken.

Her macaroni salad was probably at the top of the list. No family occasion was complete without a generous-sized bowl of Aunt Mae's macaroni salad.

While her files contained recipes for most of those dishes, there was no recipe for the macaroni salad or her hot-bacon dressing. Measurement of various ingredients was not easily accomplished because "to taste" recipes usually involved a pinch of this and a dab of that. My wife Jo Ann was not able to duplicate the macaroni salad until she found a recipe on a jar of mayonnaise.

It was easy to think that all of these recipes were family secrets that went back for generations. I'm sure there were some that we passed down to my Mother from her Mother, but I have discovered that many of my favorite family recipes were not limited to my family.

The recipe for my mom's justifiably renowned toll house cookies was on the back of a chocolate chip bag. Others were hand-written copies of ingredients and instructions for other good food ideas learned from friends and neighbors. More than a few of our perennial favorites were clipped from the pages of newspapers and magazines.

Actually, the origin of these recipes really did not matter. When made by my Mother, my Mother-in-law or my wife, the most important ingredient is love.

+++

God's love is life's essential flavor.

32 FAMILY RESEMBLANCE

Mother was at the registration window of the oncology department getting signed in for her monthly appointment. I was standing behind the wheelchair that we used to get her from the car to the second-floor cancer clinic.

Then the clerk said something that immediately caught my attention. "That must be your son," she said. "I could tell by the resemblance."

Up until that moment, I had never even considered the possibility that I looked like my Mother.

We did have the same type of fair skin, paler than pale. Other than being prone to sunburn, though, I could not think of any physical similarities between my Mother and me.

Even after I had given the comparison considerable thought, the only other trait I saw that we shared was poor eyesight.

It was after more thought that I realized that it was much more important if I resembled her spiritually.

My Mother was a kind person, whose good deeds were done as quietly as possible. She was a woman of deep faith. She visited God often in church and talked with Him continuously in prayer. She always placed her family above herself as a devoted wife and wonderful Mother, making countless sacrifices on our behalf.

On Mother's Day and all other days, I would do well to imitate my Mother's love of God and others. Only then will I be able to hope that I bear at least a slight resemblance to her.

+++

We are made in God's image;
we resemble Him only in love.

33 HEALING HANDS

If you ever saw the gnarled hands with their swollen knuckles, you would think that Mother was a prisoner of her arthritis. But she was able do a lot of good with those hands. Perhaps, her spiritual action was the physical therapy that permitted to continue to use what could have been regarded as beyond help.

Even after she developed osteoarthritis somewhere in her 40s, Mother never let the condition stop her from continuing a lifelong practice of using her hands to help others.

In retrospect, it is hard to imagine all that she did on behalf of my siblings, Dad and me. My sister Mary Jo – and her dolls – was among the best dressed in town as a result of the dresses, skirts and other outfits that Mother turned out on her Singer® sewing machine.

Later on, she took up crocheting and my siblings and I still have one or two examples of the afghans that she created.
Of course, the hands-on activity that remained nearest and dearest to our family's heart (and stomach) was Mother's cooking and baking. Her hands had little rest in the kitchen where she turned out countless meals roast beef, veal cutlets, breaded chicken and other entrees, topped off with a variety of baked goods such as crazy cake and apple roll.

Mother also used her hands to help others outside of our home. She volunteered as a runner and driver for Meals on Wheels deliveries to shut-ins. She was a pierogie pincher for quite a few years for a church. It wasn't even the one she attended.

She was always willing to lend a helping hand to those in need. She often volunteered to drive people to the hospital, doctor's office and elsewhere.

Over the years, I don't think I ever heard her complain about the arthritic pain in her fingers. She never took any kind of medication for her hands.

Well, she did in a way. I have vivid memories of her sitting on rocking chair in the living room with her crooked fingers and their swollen knuckles working their way along the beads in a countless number of rosary recitations. Equally memorable was the way her hands held the small photo album that she used to centralize various prayers and devotions she had acquired over the years.

Her deep faith was evident in her love for and devotion to God. It was also obvious in the way she lent a helping hand to others.

As Christ demonstrated on the cross, love conquers pain.

+++

**Helping others helps us
to forget our pain.**

34 GODMOTHER

Children often offer a unique point of view, prompting adults to take an uncommon look at a common word.

Such was the case for my Mother's goddaughter Bonnie Becker. Bonnie's family moved from town not long after her christening over 50 years ago. They settled in New Jersey and my mom saw her goddaughter only once in that half century or so.

However, Mother and Bonnie kept in touch by cards and letters over the years – long letters. Courtesy of the U.S. Postal Service, Mother updated Bonnie on what was happening with our family and Bonnie wrote about herself, her daughter and, eventually, her grandchildren.

Each year, the letters stated it would be nice for godmother and goddaughter to get together on a visit. As is often the case with good intentions, the years slipped by without the intention becoming reality.

Then Mother was diagnosed with a brain tumor in April. When Bonnie didn't receive Mom's customary Christmas-time letter, she called Mother's house early in the next year and we told her that Mother was in a long-term care unit at a local hospital.

Thanks to faulty directions, it took Bonnie 6 hours to make the 4-hour trip to the hospital to visit with my Mother. Bonnie's only regret was that the reunion had not come sooner.

When Bonnie returned to New Jersey, she told her grandchildren that she had been visiting her godmother. One of them, obviously a fan of Cinderella, thought she had been visiting her *fairy* godmother.

After my Mother died a few months later, we could not get in touch with Bonnie until the day before the funeral. Even with that short notice, Bonnie made it to her godmother's funeral.

Obviously, there was no fairy tale enchantment about my Mother and Bonnie's relationship. I don't think Mother even owned a magic wand.

Their tie was one of love. It was not too different from the relationship we sometimes maintain with God. We communicate only infrequently even though we intend to visit with Him more often.

If we do renew our acquaintance with God we regret all the time we wasted. However, we do rediscover God's all-encompassing love for us.

Now, that is truly magical.

+++

**The only true "magic" words
were spoken by Christ.**

35 LOVE CONNECTION

During her final 1 1/2 –year illness, my Mother received dozens of greeting cards from relatives, friends and acquaintances offering prayers and support.

The most frequent card sender was her cousin Phyllis Hershey, who sent anywhere from one to three greeting cards every week of those 18 months. Many were greeting cards that Phyllis had created by having her pressed-flower arrangements printed.

The content was both encouraging and newsy. Phyllis would write about her family and other items of daily life. She would note that members of her church and other friends were praying for Mother. She also regretted that she couldn't be with her.

Phyllis had been with Mother since childhood. She was only 2 years older than my Mother and lived in the next block, so the two were close friends as well as cousins. There are photos of the pair together as toddlers and at a party celebrating my Mother's 80th birthday.

After each was married and family responsibilities became much greater, they still managed to keep in touch with phone calls, cards and occasional visits.

Eventually, their children were grown and on their own and both women had lost their husbands to cancer and Alzheimer's disease, respectively.

Several times when Phyllis had surgery, my Mother would travel to spend a week or so to help out, play two-handed pinochle and share many laughs. My Mother would visit for several days about once a year even when Phyllis was not recuperating.

Phyllis' driving was limited to local trips, but she did not hesitate to brave the interstate and come to stay when Mother had surgery a decade or so before her brain tumor.

Their last major venture together came in 2007 a few months after my Mother had both knees replaced. She and Phyllis sailed on wonderful cruise to Alaska.

When the tumor severely limited my Mother's mobility, Phyllis paid one last visit to her lifelong friend. Her daughter drove her to my Mother's home for 1-day stay. That evening Phyllis slept on the living room sofa to be with Mother who was in a hospital bed across the room.

Even though Phyllis' cards often stated that she was upset because she could not do more for Mother, that was not quite true.

Phyllis had given her cousin and lifelong friend all that she had to give – love.

In the end, love is all we have to give God and others, and love is what God has to give us. This love is all that we truly need.

+++

**When everything is gone,
God's love remains.**

36 WORTH BY FAITH

In over eight decades of life, my Mother must have prayed for hundreds of people – from her family to casual acquaintances. So, when she was diagnosed with a malignant brain tumor, it was only fitting that hundreds of people prayed for her.

While all prayers are heard and God can do anything, I doubt that many of those who prayed believed that a miracle cure would occur. We were asking for her to have a holy and happy death.

Those prayers were answered in the diverse group of women who were her roommates when she was at a nursing home for rehabilitation and in a medical center's long-term care unit. Each of these ladies blessed her life in different ways.

At the nursing home/rehab center, Mary and Mother would enjoy themselves complaining about the food.

After being hospitalized when she broke a hip and had it replaced, she moved to the long-term unit where her first roommate was a lively 96-year-old former teacher named Agnes. She took such joy in the simple pleasures of life such as a bowl of ice cream, Mother could not but help to do the same.

Joan, who had a knee replaced, was only a roommate for a week or so, but she was fiercely protective of Mother. She made sure that the staff was aware of whatever Mother needed. She also knit her a beautiful lap robe that was almost as warm as the friendship that inspired the gift.

Then there was Marie. She was unexpectedly hospitalized for what turned out to be a very serious illness, but she never complained and was concerned about Mother's condition. She, like Joan, came to my Mother's wake even though Marie was far from well herself.

The last roommate was a lovely lady named Hazel, who was crowned with a halo of white hair. Her short-term memory had faded, but she illuminated the room by the light of her smile.

Reflecting on those last months, it becomes apparent that God not only heard those prayers on behalf of Mother – He answered them.

+++

People are often God's answers to prayers.

37 DOUBLE DIP OF LOVE

According to the old cliché "bread is the staff of life." However, in our house ice cream was the stuff that made life more enjoyable.

Our parents were hard-pressed to keep a supply of the frozen treat on hand for my two brothers, my sister and me. Ice cream was often served as a pre-bedtime snack unless someone had finished off the cartons in the freezer.

For variety, we kids would sometimes eat our bowl of ice cream by using pretzels or potato chips as utensils. Bowls and cones were supplemented by occasional ice cream sodas served in brightly colored aluminum cups or milkshakes which presented a challenge to our straws and our intake.

Our folks would also regularly lead us on walking expeditions to a small ice cream place about 6 or 7 blocks from home. Actually, it was a garage for Martz's Dairy with a small room with freezers so the attendant could dip out teaberry, white cherry, rocky road and other favorites.

Three decades later, the roles were reversed. When Dad was a patient at the Lebanon Veterans Affairs Medical Center, we would stop at a nearby convenience store to pick up a pint of ice cream for our visit to the Alzheimer's unit. We never had to worry about what to do with leftover ice cream.

A dozen years later found Mother as a patient in the long-term unit of St. Catherine's Medical Center. When my wife Jo Ann and I visited, we usually brought a container of ice cream that Mother rarely refused. My siblings would add variety when they visited by sometimes bringing her a milkshake or sundae.

I'm not sure, but ice cream might have been the last food Jo Ann fed Mother before Mother began a rapid decline that ended with her death.

What was the connection? The ice cream our parents gave us when we were growing up was an expression of their love and their desire to see us enjoy life.

The ice cream we gave our parents was an expression of our love to the two people who not only gave us life, but made it enjoyable.

+++

Love is given to others as generously as it was given to us.

38 SCARRED BY LOVE

For a guy, scars are a kind of scrapbook of skin that tell the stories of how childhood scrapes and cuts were earned. My legs have quite a few scars whose stories are lost to the years. But my right shin bears one that is more recent and more memorable.

I got that scar about 11 a.m. on Wednesday, Nov. 18, 2009. I can be that specific because it was Mother's funeral. We were carrying her casket, adorned in painted carnations, down the stone steps in front of the church when I mis-stepped and banged my shin.

Along the sides were my brothers Phil and Dave, my sister Mary Jo and our cousins, who also represented their respective spouses. My nephew Greg, the youngest of our immediate family, was at the foot of the casket while I, the new eldest member, was at the head.

As Mother's mortal remains made their final journey, they were surrounded by her nearest and dearest from youngest to oldest.

I suppose I don't need that scar on my leg to remind me of Mother's sacrifices made in faith and out of love any more than I need the scars on Jesus' hands, feet and side to remind me of what He endured on the cross for our sake.

However, the physical scar will serve to remind me that scars that loved one's leave on our souls will be erased forever when life on earth ends and life in heaven begins.

+++

God can make a scarred soul whole.

39 GIFT LIST

My parents must have had a couple dozen of tasks and chores to perform to make our childhood Christmases memorable for my brothers, sister and me. At least they did not have to worry about dusting the second-floor hallway that led to the staircase.

We kids would be up at a time when a self-respecting rooster would be hitting the snooze alarm. We would immediately be slithering on our bellies down the hall to get as close as we could to the top of the stairs to catch a glimpse of what Santa left under the tree.

Once we got the go-ahead from the folks, we would stampede down the steps at a volume that would make the Oklahoma land rush seem as quiet as a Quaker meeting.

Years later, my siblings and their families would have to assemble at the homestead to share Christmas cheer and holiday noise. The present opening was relatively tame, but the Uno® games could get a bit spirited.

One of the traditions of the latter-day Christmas family gatherings was the drawing of grownups' names out of a hat. My niece and nephews were still recipients of gifts from grandparents, aunts and uncles, but the adults' presents were limited.

Mother would pull from a hat slips of papers containing the grownups' names. We drew the name of the person to whom we would give a gift. She also recorded who had whom and kept the list handy because we all asked many times throughout the year, "Whose name do I have?"

I keep a copy of the last year we drew names, a Christmas that occurred a few months after Mother's 80th birthday. A few months after that, she learned she had a brain tumor. Christmas that year was more quiet and subdued.

Last year was our first Christmas without our Mother. It was the quietest holiday ever for our family. This Christmas will be just as subdued.

However, the quiet will give us a chance to reflect upon the J.M. Barrie quote, "God gave us memories that we might have roses in December."

Illuminated by the love heralded when Christ was born, these memories speak of the gift of family love loudly and clearly.

+++

We listen for God's love

with our hearts, not our ears

40 LOUD AND DEAR

When you visit a patient in some hospitals, you will see a whiteboard that lists the names of all the nurses, LPNs and aides on duty on that floor. Such a sign would was usually not necessary at the hospital where my Mother spent her final 9 months.

It didn't take very long after my wife Jo Ann, other visitors and I got of the elevator at the long-term care unit to find out if Maggie, an aide, was working. You could hear her long before you saw her.

Maggie's heart was a soft as her speaking voice was loud. She really cared about all the patients. Even those who could not speak well or whose minds had withered knew that she cared for them. As an added bonus, she was one person deaf patients did not have to ask to speak up.

Maggie might have been a bit louder than most of the people who took care of my Mother during her 18-month-long struggle with a brain tumor, but her dedication was typical. Whether in a nursing home, hospital or in my mom's home, virtually all the nurses, LPNs and aides coupled care with compassion – throwing in a dash of love.

After years of daily visits to see her Father in a nursing home, my wife Jo Ann is convinced it takes a special type of person who helps those who cannot help themselves.

Sooner or later, many of us are faced with a situation where we pray to God to help a loved one who is critically ill. Often, our request for a healing is not granted.

However, Maggie and other caring professionals like her are likely to be the answer that God does give.

+++

Love speaks volumes.

41 IN THEIR IMAGE

When a loved one is afflicted with medical problems that require him or her to be hospitalized, receive home health care or be placed in a long-term care facility, it is only natural to pray to God so that the person would be returned to good health.

When Dad was a patient in an Alzheimer's unit at a VA medical center and when Mother was in the long-term unit at a medical center in the final stage of a brain tumor, we knew that neither would be restored – at least in this life.

That still did not prevent us from wishing that the people who were taking care of our parents could have known them as we and others knew them before their health declined.

Dad was a very intelligent educator who taught advanced math, physics and social studies, and who served as guidance counselor, acting superintendent and assistant high school principal. He loved to read, but he loved to smile and joke just as much.

Once she recovered from raising my two brothers and me and getting our sister well-started in school, Mother returned to the work force as a part-time clerk at the local JC Penney's Store. When the store was closed, she did not sit at home.

She loved to travel and had many a memorable trip with Dad. Later, she was a regular on chartered bus tours to musicals and places of interest. She also loved to laugh and to make others laugh.

Both were very giving and both were people of deep faith in God. Faith came first, family second and all other aspects of life after those. Both parents tried to help others. Dad donated over 13 gallons of blood, and Mother volunteered to deliver Meals on Wheels and help parishioners of another church make pierogies.

Their final care givers may have caught the merest idea of what kind of people Mother and Dad were before they became sick. Dad still had his endearing smile, which spoke for him when his words became as jumbled as his thoughts. Mother could still laugh even when the tumor nearly eliminated her ability to talk.

It is up to us, their daughter, sons, daughters-in-law, son-in-law and grandchildren to recall what they were like – and to try to live to their standards of faith and love.

+++

**We are known by
the good that we inspire.**

42 WRAPPED IN PRAYER

My sister has been friends with Tricia for about 30 years even since they met as students at Lock Haven University. They have many things in common, including the example of strong Mothers. Tricia's Mom Frances and Mary Jo's Mother were the anchors of love, hope and strength of their families.

When Mother became ill, Tricia, her husband Ernie and her Mom sent Mother a prayer shawl of blue, Mother's favorite color. The card that accompanied the knitted, powder blue gift read, "My Mom made this prayer shawl for you. I hope it gives you a little bit of peace and comfort knowing that you are in our prayers."

The shawl was begun and finished with prayer. Such shawls have many purposes. Weddings, grief, birthdays, illness and births are just a few of its uses. Ultimately, there would be another purpose.

The shawl was kept on the back of the chair where Mother sat and used frequently while she was able to remain at home.

After Mother died, the shawl was put to another use. During her final illness, her skin became almost as thin and fragile as butterfly's wings. Nurses and aides were extremely careful and kind, but even their tender care could not prevent Mother from getting skin tears on her arms.

This posed a problem. Mother's final outfit – blue, of course – was a dress with short sleeves. The funeral director was concerned that he would not be able to conceal the skin tears even with makeup.

That's when Mary Jo had the inspired idea of completing Mother's outfit with the prayer shawl.

Our final image of Mother's earthly body was one of her wrapped in the knitted love of the prayer shawl with a rosary in her hands.

In the beginning, the prayer shawl was a hand-knit, heart-felt gift of love. In the, it was a prayer of love, hope and strength from one Mother to another.

+++

Love knits us all together.

43 SKIPPY

For over 80 years, Mother had one nickname – "Mae." She was the namesake of her own Mother, so her nickname helped avoid the confusion that two Marys in one household would have caused.

It wasn't until her final illness that she acquired another nickname – "Skippy."

The new name did not rival Mae or even Aunt Mae in popularity. In fact, the only person who called her "Skippy" was Diane, an aide from Family Home Health Medical.

Diane was one a group of dedicated nurses and aides who helped her as the tumor began to severely limit what Mother could do. They were also there for her when she was able to return from the nursing home to spend a final three months in her home of 50 years.

Family Home Health Medical lives up to its motto, "Our clients become family."

Diane and the other care givers took care of our Mother as if she were their Mother. More than a few went above and beyond the call of duty, including two who stopped on their own time and with small treats to visit Mother on Christmas Day.

Virtually all of the aides and nurses were special, but Diane was probably the most. It was she who spent the most time with Mother.

Diane also shared something special with Mother – laughter. Mother always enjoyed laughing and using her Irish wit to get others laughing. However, as the brain tumor progressed, she had less and less reason to laugh.

The cancer robbed her of ability to speak clearly, and its stroke-like paralysis of her right side slowly robbed her of the ability to do even the most basic tasks such as feeding herself and grooming.

However, she and Diane always seemed to find something to laugh about. This sometimes turned what could have been an embarrassing moment into something that was genuinely funny. The humor they shared helped to brighten up the day.

God's simplest gifts are His greatest. Such is the case in laughter.

That was the case with Diane and Mae – Skippy.

+++

Compassion by any other name would be just as sweet.

44 JOYFUL MUSIC

One of my most vivid childhood memories is of Mother singing as she went about the arduous tasks of cooking for and cleaning up after three sons and a daughter. Her melodious voice would float sweetly through the air throughout the day.

Unfortunately, genetics failed miserably when it came to me inheriting a good singing voice – or even a so-so one. Let's put it this way: I always sing alone. There may be people in the room when I start, but by the time I get done I'm alone.

Despite this lack of vocal talent and a similar ineptitude in instrumental music, I was encouraged when my folks showed whenever I performed with the school chorus or played in a band concert. They even endured my accordion practicing without the benefit of earplugs.

Once I got out of school, I decided not to press my luck and confined my singing to a well-soundproofed shower.

It has only been in recent years that I've become more vocal – fortunately only in private, though.

I don't know the reason for this. Maybe it was a delayed reaction to the words of a former pastor who quoted a saint who noted that by singing hymns we pray twice. Maybe it is an overflow of joy that faith has brought me.

It took a while to build up a repertoire, since I was more inclined to learn the lyrics to pop songs than hymns in the days when I sang regularly. So I had to memorize new songs, a line or two each day, until I knew enough that I wouldn't sound like a broken, badly scratched record.

Now, I know enough songs to carry me through various activities at the house and I've found they help brighten up even the darkest of days.

One of the more recent additions was "Joyful, Joyful, We Adore Thee," a song which my family had requested as the closing hymn for my Dad's funeral Mass.

I wasn't too familiar with Henry Van Dyke's beautiful words to Beethoven's most uplifting melody, but I learned them line by line, verse by verse until I came to the end of the fourth and final verse.

My singing voice still isn't any better than it was, but my insights have improved.

Joyful music does indeed lift us "Sonward" and out of the trials of life.

And God – like our parents – hears with his heart not his ears, so all our music – no matter what its quality – is pleasing to Him.

+++

Singing God's praises is always joyful.

45 DANCE OF LOVE

Our Mother and Dad loved to dance. With four kids to raise, they didn't get many opportunities to "trip the light fantastic," but they took advantage of the rare nights out, as well as wedding receptions and other social gatherings.

Foxtrots and waltzes were in their repertoire, but the polka was their favorite. Their favorite polka musician was accordionist Johnny Bogush and his group, but they would polka with equal enthusiasm even if it were to a record of *She's Too Fat for Me* spun by a disc jockey.

Dad, who at his peak packed 260-plus pounds on his 6-3 frame, was surprisingly spry and light on his feet. Mother blended in perfectly despite the arthritis that eventually led her to get replacement knees.

People enjoyed watching them dance even after Dad's brilliant mind began to be eaten away by Alzheimer's disease.

Most memorable and meaningful to the family were the times they danced at the wedding receptions of their sons and new daughters-in-law – first Dave and Holly, then Phil and Helen and finally me and Jo Ann.

Dad did not live long enough to fulfill a Father's wish to dance at the wedding of his daughter Mary Jo and her husband Holden.

There was one, somewhat unusual aspect to Mother's dancing – she would politely refuse requests from other men for a dance. She would only dance with Dad.

As Dad's illness progressed, Mother did not have time for dancing even if she did have the inclination. Alzheimer's steadily eroded his mental ability. However, a lifelong habit of walking all around the town and to and from the high school where he taught made him a hard guy to keep up with.

That was one of the problems. Mother could help Dad's confusion when he was at home, but he could be out the door and blocks away before she even realized he was gone. One day, a couple brought Dad home. They had seen him walking along the highway several miles away on the other side of a sizable mountain.

Eventually, Dad became a patient in an Alzheimer's unit at Lebanon VA Medical Center. He and Mother would walk through the hallways of the huge complex and on the beautiful campus. When his condition took a major turn for the worse and he was confined to a geriatric chair, Mother was by his side.

A dozen years after Dad's death, Mother's brain tumor was discovered. A lifetime of being on the go, taking care of her family and helping others gave her physical and spiritual stamina she needed to follow God's will, but the tumor put more and more restrictions on how she could get around.

Then on Nov. 15, 2009, two days before what would have been Dad's 89th birthday, she slipped silently from earthly to eternal life.

According to the old song, *In Heaven There Is No Beer*.

I doubt that there are polkas in Heaven, but I am certain Mother is reunited with her only dance partner. Her and Dad's illnesses have danced away in the melody of God's and their own love song.

+++

The song of love never ends.

46 PATCHWORK OF LOVE

The sentiments contained in sympathy cards a family receives after the death of a loved one often provide a different perspective of that person when they are assembled mosaic-like.

"Mae was a wonderful woman and I will never forget how nice she was to me and my family. My Mother simply adored her all through her life. They are all together now in heaven..."

"I've made a donation...in memory of your beloved Mother, my dearest friend."

"She truly was a blessing for you and the community. Her spirit will continue to be with you always."

"I'll always remember your Mother and what a lovely woman she was. I'll especially remember her asking me about my family and helping me out whenever I was in J.C. Penney."

"She was a wonderful person and I feel privileged to know have known her."

"I will always remember her as a kind and gentle lady. She was always nice to me. When I first came to Mount Carmel, she was work at Penney's. My English was very, very poor and she always helped me out."

"I've known your Mother for many years. I did part-time at Penney's when I first met her on the second floor in 1955...Phyllis is a close friend of mine and shared the times when she (Mother) came to Phyl's. It was always a privilege to be with her."

"I loved your Mother's sense of humor and her great laugh! She will be greatly missed!"

"What a special person your Mother was!"

"Your Mother was a wonderful person and I am so glad that I had the privilege to know her."

"I will always remember her as having a smile for everyone."

"Your Mother was a wonderful woman!"

"I will always remember the good times we had together – shopping, playing cards and eating pizza."

"When my daughter was a 'pre-teen,' she had a slight weight problem. A first-time slumber party disaster was avoided because of the words of wisdom from your Mother. Not only did she find the appropriate nightgown for her, gave her wisdom gems, but she also slipped a dollar bill into her hand! What a woman, what a life, what a Mother!!"

"Your dear Mom was such a special lady. I will always remember her smiling face and kind way she had. She really lived life to the fullest."

"I have great memories of wonderful times together with Mae! A lifetime of great childhood – being raised on the same street. My friends here asked about her all the time…She brought lots of fun wherever she visited.

"I know her family is very proud of her and the whole town will remember all she participated in – she was everything from a politician to a pierogie maker. We love her dearly."

+++

Each life touches the lives of many.

47 THINKING OF HER

At home, in hospitals and in nursing homes, Mother received dozens of cards and notes offering get-well wishes or just letting her know they had not forgotten her.

The most prolific of these card senders was her cousin Phyllis Hershey, but Mother received sentiments from a variety of people in her life.

One note came from her goddaughter Bonnie Becker after she traveled from New Jersey to visit Mother in the long-term care unit at St. Catherine's Medical Center.

"I can't begin to tell you just how happy I was to see you and visit with you," Bonnie wrote. "I deeply regret all the years that have gone by – a lifetime. Though we have not seen each other in all these many years, you are a very important part of my life, and _always_ have been. I have thoroughly enjoyed our correspondence and looked forward to your letters and cards…Stay well and know that you are always in my thoughts and prayers."

"How we enjoyed our many 2-handed pinochle games – about 25 a day," wrote Phyllis about Mother's occasional visits. "If we had a lull, Mae would say, 'Sit down" and she'd start dealing…

"My friends always enjoyed her visits, too. Saturday nights she would go to the Good Shepherd Catholic Church and then on Sunday to my church."

"Our prayers and hugs are with you daily," wrote one of Phyllis' friends, who signed off her note, "Love and memories."

Another cousin wrote, *"I always remember the great dinners you would make for us when we would come to visit and how funny your Joe would be...We love you and want the best for you."*

"Grandma Mae, I pray for people as good as you are to enter people's lives daily," wrote Christian. *"I know you'll make it through this, and I wait eagerly for the next time I may see you!"*

Then there was a card from a long-time acquaintance, who taught at the high school where Dad taught. *"...A former student told me you are at St. Catherine's. I know this is a difficult time, and I want you to know that I care. You are in my prayers."*

Another writer was Betty Menapace, who was Mother's roommate on a dream tour of Ireland, the home of Mother's Graham ancestors. *"I think of you often and remember our three weeks in Ireland. What a trip and what a great roommate I had to make it so special."*

In another card she also wrote, *"Just dropping a note to let you know you are in my prayers, novenas and all the little candles burning in the church. P.S. Remember the happy days of Ireland."*

+++

**Life is colored
by many shades of love**

48 BE IT EVER SO HUMBLE

It was a strange feeling walking through the house at 234 W. Second St. for the last time. After all, it had been our family's home for 51 years.

Footsteps were not the only sounds that echoed off the walls in the empty rooms. There were a half-century's worth of laughter, birthday and holiday parties, family meals, live music from accordions, recorded music of all kinds, occasional loud "discussions" and, most rarely, the sounds of crying.

Mother had been in a long-term care facility for nearly 9 months before my siblings and I decided to put the house on the market. The real estate agent did a good job and found a prospective buyer within a few weeks, telling us that if everything went as planned the deal would be closed on Nov. 15, 2009.

We had already started to share the acquisitions of a lifetime, donating whatever clothing and furniture that we could not use ourselves.

The closing date remained on the distant horizon until we got a call from the real estate agent telling us that Nov. 15 was a Sunday, so the buyers wanted to close the deal on Friday, Nov. 15. The intervening days passed in a blur as we packed and move in a flurry of activity.

The deal closed Friday afternoon, but we still were not done. The new buyers were moving in Saturday afternoon as we were still moving items out.

The pressure and stress of the last-minute moving were aggravated tenfold by the fact that Mother's condition had taken a sharp turn for the worse that week.

Mother died on Sunday, Nov. 15, the date we had been told would see the completion the final sale of the family homestead.

The passing of someone who, along with our Dad, had been the spirit of love in our household made the sale of the property seem insignificant by comparison.

With Mother not there anymore, it was just a house and not a home.

God's home, our home, is filled with love.

49 THE KIDS

There are few places a 50some-year-old guy can go and still be thought of as a kid. One such place is his parents' home.

In the case of my brothers and our quite-a-bit-younger sister, we were still called "kids" by Mother whenever we visited the family homestead at 234 W. Second St. Just to be clear, though, she did not treat as kids; she just referred to us as such.

My wife would pop next door on our nightly visits and sometimes Mother would be on the phone. "The kids just came in," she would tell the caller as she said good-bye to the caller and welcomed us.

My siblings were scattered over three states and the closest one lived about an hour's drive away, so their visits were usually less frequent the farther away they lived. Thus, Mother's Mother would tell her friends a week or so in advance that "My kids are coming home."

My brother Phil summed up the situation almost poetically.

"We were so very blessed to have her as a Mother. She took great pride in everything we did and loved hearing our stories.

"I will never forget the image of her sitting in her chair in the dining room waiting for our arrival home. I'd like to picture her in the same chair in Heaven, waiting for us when we arrive some day."

To her, were always her kids and always will be her kids. To us, she was and always will be our Mother.

We hope that someday she will be able to say, "My kids are coming home."

+++

We are all God's children.

50 LIFE'S END AND BEGINNING

When I got home from school that day in early October 2008, there was a message for me to call Mother's oncologist. I was more than a bit apprehensive when I called the oncology department and I got to speak to the doctor almost immediately.

The news, as expected, was not good. The doctor said the chemotherapy and radiation that they began to use in mid May were no longer working. Mother's brain tumor was growing.

Next, I had to ask the question I wished I did not need to ask: What was her prognosis?

The doctor did not hesitate. He estimated that she had about 6 months to live.

The only comforting thought came when I asked him about what pain she could expect. Thanks be God, she had not experience any pain from the tumor yet. He said that if she did not have pain by then, she probably would not have it.

Six months came and went; so did the anniversary of my conversation with the doctor. Mother had an increasingly hard time getting around and her speech became ever-more-difficult to understand, but she still had a good appetite, no pain, and both reason and ability to laugh.

She was able to spend Christmas 2008 in her home; however, she broke her hip the morning of Dec. 31. After she was discharged from the hospital where she received a hip replacement, she was transferred to the long-term care unit of St. Catherine's Medical Center and spent her last 11 months there.

The end came will shocking and numbing suddenness. On our visit Wednesday evening, Jo Ann was able to help Mother eat her dessert. By the next day, the nurses and aides had a hard time getting her to eat anything.

Each day, it seemed as though she faded a bit more. When Jo Ann was able to visit Mother with me on Saturday, she was shocked by how much Mother's health had declined.

Late Sunday morning, Nov. 15, 2009, the registered nurse on Mother's floor called to tell me that her condition was critical. "It could be hours; it could be days," she said.

We called my brothers Phil and Dave, and my sister Mary Jo to relay the sad news. Phil planned to come in Monday from his home in New York. Dave would be kept updated in Ohio. Mary Jo and her husband Holden would meet us at the hospital.

They got there early Sunday afternoon, not long after Jo Ann and I had arrived. Mother slept peacefully throughout the afternoon until the fall sky darkened into evening. Around 6 p.m., Mary Jo suggested that we contact a priest.

We knew our and my Mother's pastor was out of town, so we called the other pastor from our town as a backup in case we could not reach the medical center's Catholic chaplain. When we inquired about the chaplain, we learned the hospital no longer had one and we called the Very Rev. Frank Karwacki again. He immediately agreed to make the trip to anoint Mother.

Father Frank arrived at room 258 shortly after 7 p.m., anointing Mother and giving her a final blessing. Father Frank, who was on the faculty with our Dad before father had a calling to enter the priesthood, stayed and chatted with us for about 20 minutes after the blessing.

It was about 8:30 p.m. when Jo Ann and I said we were leaving to visit her Mom and Mary Jo and Holden went out to get something to eat.

Mary Jo and Holden were back in the room briefly before Mother's shallow breathing quietly ceased altogether.

En route home from Jo Ann's Mom's home, we got the call from my brother Dave.

When we returned to the hospital, we received the condolences of teary-eyed aides and nurse before entering the room where Mary Jo And Holden were still waiting.

We prayed our good-bye and kissed Mother a last time.

Her long journey had ended.

Her life reunited with Dad, those she loved and the God Who had been the core of her soul had begun.

+++

Our journey on life takes us to our ultimate destination.

51 ONE IN LOVE

Dad, Joseph W. Kozlowski, was not quite 7 years old on Sunday, Sept. 4, 1927. That was the date when his future wife and our future mother, Mary P. "Mae" Krouch, was born on the other side of town.

They spent the better part of the next 20 years moving in separate orbits. He was almost out of Our Mother of Consolation School before she began at Our Lady's School. He started his junior year at Bloomsburg State Teachers College about the time she was an incoming freshman at Mount Carmel Catholic High School. While she was finishing up high school and getting started in the work force, he was a member of the U.S. Navy Seabees in the South Pacific during World War II and then a newly hired high school physics teacher.

Eventually, though, they met through a mutual friend named Flo Kakiel. They were married June 9, 1948, and parted only by dad's summer school studies as a high school teacher and, much later, his hospitalization due to Alzheimer's disease.

Dad died Sept. 29, 1996, a few weeks after his wife's birthday. When she was diagnosed with a brain tumor about 12 years later, mother's healthy lifestyle enabled her to live months past her oncologist's prognosis.

Mother's health began to fail rapidly in the second week of November 2009. When the nurse told us that she had only days to live, I suppose all my siblings and I thought she might die on Nov. 17, dad's birthday. Her decline was even more rapid than supposed, and she died on Nov. 15.

His date of death nearly coincided with her birthday; her date of death was 2 days away from his birthday.

Their deep love for each other and their family was a natural outcome of their deep love of God.

This love was such that the days of their births and of their deaths blended to form their endless days together in God's presence.

+++

Death is the door from earthly love to eternal love.

52 ALLELUJAH!

The "alleluias" of Easter were still echoing in the air when we got the news in the shadows and glare of a hospital emergency cubicle. Our Mother's slightly slurred speech was not from a mild stroke. It was the symptom of a brain tumor.

Up until that April 1st afternoon, my Mother looked and kept on the go like a woman 20 years younger than her 80 years. She exercised regularly and volunteered often, a regimen that kept her physically fit. Her spiritual fitness came from attending church regularly, serving as a Eucharistic special minister several times a month and spending hours in prayer daily.

The disease and its treatment took a heavy toll in the past year and a half on all aspects of her life – even the spiritual. First, she had to stop serving as a special minister and attending Mass, but she maintained her daily prayer habits. After a few months, she no longer read her prayer books, but she still said the Rosary. Before we said good-bye each night, we had to make sure her Rosary beads were near her.

Eventually, she could no longer "say" her prayers. Instead, her entire life became a prayer.

The extent of her spiritual strength during this – the worst of years – was most evident in what she did not do even once during her illness of 19 months – complain to others or question God.

Part of her head had to be shaved for a brain biopsy. She underwent 30 radiation treatments, and a month of chemotherapy and several more rounds. She spent time in three different hospitals and underwent rehabilitation in two nursing homes. As if the tumor were not enough, she broke her hip on the last day of 2008 and had to have that replaced.

Through all those trials, she never complained about her physical health or pain. She did not ask God why she, His faithful servant, had to suffer.

After all, how could she complain if Jesus, her Savior, did not when He willingly underwent the agony of the Crucifixion? He knew that His suffering killed death and purchased Heaven for all of His followers.

That is why Mae Kozlowski, our Mother, is hearing the "alleluias" of Easter and seeing God, the object of that joyful exclamation. The only difference is that those "alleluias" will not fade; they will ring out for her and her loved ones forever.

+++

God transforms tears of sorrow
into tears of joy.

EPILOGUE

When a loved one passes away, people share a bit of your grief through the expression of condolences. This was the case when my Mother passed away.

According to "Online Etymology Dictionary," the word condole comes from the Latin word "condolere" that means "to suffer together." People shared our grief in a variety of ways.

There were kind words offered at the funeral home and after the funeral Mass. There were pleasant memories shared. There were touching sympathy cards. There were memorial donations to my mother's church and the public library.

The most poignant condolence, though, was left on our answering machine by our "nephew" Ryan, who was a first grader in an elementary school. His quiet, little voice spoke the following:

"Aunt Jo Ann and Uncle Walt, I'm sorry your Mom passed away. I've been thinking about you. I love you so much. I'm sorry your Mom passed away. I've been thinking about you. I'll call back. Bye. Love you. Ryan."

When my wife talked to Ryan's mom about the message, his mother said that Ryan wanted to call when he heard her and his grandmother talking about my mother's death but she had no idea of what he was going to say.

Ryan is too young to even know what the word "condolence" is defined as in a dictionary. However, he is not too young to realize that we can share God's love with those who are grieving or suffering most.

+++

God's love is always with us.

ABOUT THE AUTHOR

Walt Kozlowski is school library media specialist, and teaches English and U.S. history at Mount Carmel Area Junior-Senior High School, Mount Carmel, PA. He writes two weekly columns in The News-Item, Shamokin, PA. *Saturday's Spirit* is an inspirational column that was the source for many of the preceding chapters. That has appeared since 1995. *Walt's Way*, a humor column, has been published since March 13, 1986. He worked as a staff writer and later assistant editor for The News-Item before he became a teacher in 2000. He is blessed to have been married to the former Jo Ann Veach since Sept. 7, 1991.

AUTHOR'S NOTE

Please excuse the missed words, typographical errors and other mistakes that appear in this book. Computer engineers have devised spell check and grammar check, but they have yet to develop software that writes what I really intended to write. I appreciate your forgiveness.

The pictures on the front and back covers were taken on Mother's cruise to Alaska 3 months before her 80th birthday in 2007. The front cover photo is of her with her beloved cousin Phyllis Hershey.

WJK

www.ingramcontent.com/pod-product-compliance
Lightning Source LLC
Chambersburg PA
CBHW071318040426
42444CB00009B/2042